D1083180

MEGASTARS™

THE JONAS BROTHERS

TAMRA ORR

rosen publishing's
rosen central®

New York

Published in 2011 by The Rosen Publishing Group, Inc.
29 East 21st Street, New York, NY 10010

First Edition

Library of Congress Cataloging-in-Publication Data

Orr, Tamra.
The Jonas Brothers/Tamra Orr. — 1st ed.
    p. cm. — (Megastars)
Includes bibliographical references, discography, and index.
ISBN 978-1-4358-3572-6 (library binding)
ISBN 978-1-4488-2258-4 (pbk.)
ISBN 978-1-4488-2264-5 (6-pack)
1. Jonas Brothers–Juvenile literature. 2. Rock musicians–United States–Biography–Juvenile literature. I. Title.
ML3930.J62O77 2011
782.42164092'2–dc22
[B]
                                                                    2010026864

Manufactured in the United States of America

CPSIA Compliance Information: Batch #W11YA: For further information, contact Rosen Publishing, New York, New York, at 1-800-237-9932.

On the cover: Nick, Joe, and Kevin Jonas have sold more than eight million albums worldwide.

CONTENTS

INTRODUCTION

It is hard to imagine, when looking at the dark, curly locks of the Jonas Brothers, that their entire careers started with a haircut—but it is true. The turning point that would shift the boys from just being three brothers with the last name of Jonas to the Jonas Brothers, world-famous rock stars and teen idols, occurred at the local hair salon.

The plan was to stop and get six-year-old Nicholas Jonas a quick haircut. Denise and her son had to wait their turn, and it didn't take long before Nicholas was feeling bored.

Everyone in his family knew that he sang whenever he got the chance. It was just who he was and what he did. "Singing is my life," Nicholas says in the book *Just Jonas!* "I think I have always known that. It's just something that since I can remember, I knew. That is something that everybody always says, but for me it is true. From the age of two, I was telling my grandma I had to practice because I was going to be on Broadway."

The other women in the salon didn't know about Nick's reputation. When this little boy began belting out show tunes, everyone in the salon paid attention. It was clear that, besides being enthusiastic, Nick Jonas was also extremely talented. The amazed stylist encouraged his mother to get in touch with another customer whose son was acting in the stage musical *Les Miserables*.

Nick was thrilled to find out that someone wanted to hear him sing. He nagged his mother to contact the woman whose son was in the musical. Soon Nick had an appointment with talent agent Shirley Grant. When she heard his voice, she knew she had found a treasure. She began sending Nick out on casting calls.

Since Nick lived in Wyckoff, New Jersey, less than an hour's commute to New York City, he was able to try out for some amazing Broadway roles. He got parts in a number of plays, including Chip in *Beauty and the Beast*, Tiny Tim in *A Christmas Carol*, Little Jake in the revival of *Annie Get Your Gun*, and Kurt von Trapp in *The Sound of Music*. He even won the role of the Gavorche in *Les Miserables*, a very young revolutionary who sings several numbers before giving his life for the cause.

By the age of nine, Nicholas Jonas had already performed in some of Broadway's most popular plays. He was well known in the theater world, but not in the music world. All of that was about to change, however. Nicholas's father, Kevin, wrote and sang a song called "Joy to the World (A Christmas Prayer)." It was included on the 2002 annual *Broadway Equity Fights AIDS* CD. Nicholas sang the song again for a demo recording, which attracted the attention of INO Records, an independent Christian recording company. INO Records signed Nicholas.

A few months later, in 2002, Nicholas released his first album. Played only by Christian radio stations, it did not sell very many copies. This could have been disappointing for young Nicholas, but far bigger and better things were waiting around the corner for him—and for the rest of his family.

CHAPTER 1
A FAMILY FULL OF MUSIC

As newlyweds, Kevin Jonas Sr. and his wife, Denise, traveled from one small city to another up and down the East Coast, singing and sharing their Christian faith with others. Between Kevin's musical ability and Denise's sign language skills, they were able to minister to many, including the hearing impaired. Although the Jonases were not aware of it, this would be good practice for the life that was waiting for them a few years down the road.

In 1987, the two became parents for the first time. Their son Paul Kevin Jonas was born on November 5. His brothers followed every few years. Joseph Adam arrived on August 15, 1989; Nicholas Jerry on September 16, 1992; and Frankie Nathaniel on September 28, 2000. During this time, the family moved several times. While Denise stayed home with their sons, Kevin Sr. was often working two jobs to support his family. He was also directing a music group that demanded the family spend several months at a time on the road. It was not easy to juggle demanding work and raise small children on a tight budget, but the Jonas clan pulled through.

INSPIRATION

Kevin Sr. had been the president of the Christian Songwriters' Association but eventually became the music director of the

Christian Faith Network and then the pastor of a church. Finally, the family settled in Wyckoff, a town in northeastern New Jersey. The family lived in the parsonage, a house attached to the church. The church had a stage, which inspired the young Jonas boys to perform.

"It had a stage—an awesome stage with a full drum set and platforms," recalls Kevin Jr. in *Jonas Brothers Forever*. "It was full of music all the time, and that's where we all learned about

THE FOURTH JONAS

Believe it or not, there is a fourth Jonas Brother. Frankie Nathaniel Jonas, often referred to as Frank the Tank or the Bonus Jonas, is the youngest of the four boys. He is the only one who isn't in the family band—at least so far. That does not mean he isn't musical: he plays the guitar and has started his own band called Drop/Slap.

Since the Jonas family travels everywhere together, Frankie knows all about setting up the soundstage, doing sound checks, and all of the other hard work that goes into preparing for a concert. But instead of warming up his vocal cords like his older brothers, he usually spends his time riding his scooter around backstage.

As he gets older, Frankie Jonas is spending a growing amount of time in the spotlight. His voice was used in a documentary about the making of the Japanese movie Ponyo, *and he appeared in the Jonas film* Living the Dream. *He played Frankie Lucas in several episodes of the television show* Jonas. *He has popped up on* Entertainment Tonight *and at the*

performances and singing . . . Our mom and dad really helped us with our music and this was the place we celebrated music together." In addition to working at the church, Kevin Sr. also taught songwriting at a local Bible college, while Denise worked in the school's registrar's office. The Jonas Brothers grew up surrounded by music. Everyone in the family sang songs, played instruments, and wrote lyrics. They were greatly inspired by their father and his musical talent.

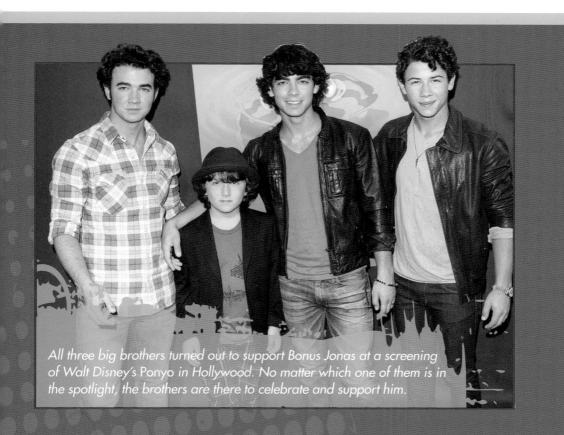

All three big brothers turned out to support Bonus Jonas at a screening of Walt Disney's Ponyo in Hollywood. No matter which one of them is in the spotlight, the brothers are there to celebrate and support him.

Nickelodeon Kids' Choice Awards. In 2010, he appeared in the movies Camp Rock: The Final Jam *and* Walter the Farting Dog. *Chances are he will be a show business fixture as he gets older—after all, it's a family tradition!*

FASCINATED BY MUSIC

Nicholas began singing around the age of two. He made stages out of coffee tables and used a turkey baster for a microphone. When he got a little older, he would make concert tickets out of construction paper and then sell them to his family. People who came to his basement concerts were treated to an entertaining show of song and dance.

His brothers were not as fascinated by music yet. When Kevin Jr. was growing up, he spent more time playing games like cowboys and Indians. His younger brothers would often join in the game, and they spent a lot of time together. "We were all really close in age, and we got along really well," says brother Joe in *Jonas Brothers Forever*. "We were each other's best friends, practically. Any chance we got, we really hung out with each other."

According to his brothers, Nicholas was singing almost from the day he was born. He

Because their faith is a large part of their lives, the Jonas Brothers sometimes perform special church concerts. Here, they perform at the Saddleback Church's Easter services at Angel Stadium.

sang absolutely everywhere he went. All of that changed the day Joe went with his younger brother to an audition. Nicholas was trying out for the lead role in the Broadway musical *Oliver!* When he finished auditioning, he came out and told Joe that the producers wanted him to try out for the role of the Artful Dodger, a talented pickpocket who is the leader of a group of child thieves. Nicholas got the part, and from that moment forward, he realized he'd found his life's calling.

A SHOWBIZ FAMILY

It was soon apparent that the three boys were headed for careers on the stage. Kevin Sr. and Denise spent a great deal of time and effort

Wherever the Jonas Brothers go, their parents are usually not far behind. The family spends time together whenever they can—even if it is between concerts.

driving their sons to and from auditions. Despite the fact that their boys were getting a lot of attention, Kevin Sr. and Denise made sure to raise them normally. Denise recently told *Parade* magazine that the boys grew up making their own beds, putting away their clothes, and performing other common household chores. They still do so today, despite being megastars. Keeping their children grounded in reality was a high priority for the Jonases.

To help with this, they began homeschooling all of their children. This way the boys had more time to get to auditions, but their parents could still make sure that the boys kept up with their studies. It also helped ensure that the brothers' education in Christian values would remain strong—a quality that makes them unique in Hollywood. In addition, according to Denise Jonas, she and her husband focused on studying each one of the boys to understand the best way to raise them based on their individual personalities. They knew that each child required his own approach. "We also emphasized consistency, boundaries, high standards, and constantly reinforced good conduct until it was behavior," Denise told *Parade* after being named ambassador for iMom, a nonprofit organization geared to helping women become better mothers.

Nicholas was the first Jonas brother to get his foot in the door and receive a recording contract. However, after his album with INO Records had disappointing sales, the family wondered what he was going to do next. The answer appeared in the form of a man named Steve Greenberg, the new president of Columbia Records. He heard songs from the *Nicholas Jonas* CD and recognized talent. "I heard that voice and I thought, 'This is the best young person's voice I've heard since Taylor Hanson. I've got to meet this guy,'" Greenberg told *Details* magazine in 2005. He was shocked—and delighted—to find out that Nicholas had two brothers who also loved to sing. When Greenberg heard all three of them together, he knew that they would be a hit.

Greenberg hired the brothers, and they began writing, performing, and recording songs together. Finally, they completed their first album, *It's About Time*. They decided to

call it that because the majority of the songs dealt with different perspectives on time. The first single on it was called "Mandy," and it was based on the true story of a girl the Jonas family knew well.

"Mandy" was also filmed as a three-part music video and show for MTV's *TRL*. The star of the video was none other than Mandy, the family's friend. Young fans loved it and wanted to hear more.

Although the brothers were busy performing their songs, their album had not come out yet. The release date kept getting pushed

Screaming female fans are a regular part of the Jonas Brothers' lives. With their love songs and good looks, it is no surprise that millions of girls follow the boys wherever they go.

back. February 2006 became March. March became April. The months kept going by. Although their songs were appearing in movies like *Aquamarine* and on TV shows like *American Dragon: Jake Long*, people were not able to buy the CD and take it home.

KEEPING BUSY

Of course, while they were waiting for the album to be released, the Jonas Brothers kept busy. They were hired as the spokespeople for a series of commercials for the candy Baby Bottle Pops. They also went on a three-month-long U.S. tour, appearing everywhere from

At Disney, the bands support and promote each other. At the Radio Disney Totally 10 Birthday Concert at Arrowhead Pond in Anaheim, California, the Jonas Brothers introduce the band Everlife.

large theaters to small clubs and city fairgrounds. Although being on tour in a rock band might seem glamorous, it was extremely exhausting. The family would pile into the family bus and often drive all night to get from one performance to the next. They did all of their own sound checks and set up all of their own equipment. Between shows, they stayed in inexpensive hotels. Although it was hard work, they had a great time.

They opened for a number of other artists, including Kelly Clarkson, Jesse McCartney, the Backstreet Boys, and Click Five. When performing a series of anti-drug concerts at public schools, they often had to be awake and on the way to their location by 5 AM. Despite the grueling schedule, the Jonas Brothers wanted to do these tours to spread the message that kids don't need to use drugs or alcohol in order to have a good time.

By the time the album was finally released in August 2006, it did not make as big an impact as everyone had hoped.

A REAL HIGH SCHOOL MUSICAL

Eastern Christian High School is a small private school in North Haledon, New Jersey. Only a few hundred students are enrolled in it. Its overall focus is a program called Faith in Action. It demands that each student spend a certain number of hours volunteering within the community before he or she is allowed to graduate. Famous graduates include actresses Katie Sagona and Antonique Smith, and Alex Noyes, the drummer for the band Honor Society.

Both Kevin and Joe attended the high school for a few years before being homeschooled by their parents. Soon after they signed a contract with Hollywood Records, however, the Jonas Brothers decided that they wanted to give back to their school and community in some way. They decided to return to Eastern Christian High School and give a free concert for all of the students.

Gary Marsh, Disney Channel Worldwide's president, is thrilled to have these talented young men on his network. With the success of Camp Rock, he is even happier.

Columbia did very little marketing or advertising for the album, which was released in limited numbers. When another single, "Year 3000," started being played on Radio Disney, the fans of the Jonas Brothers clamored for more. Unfortunately, Steve Greenberg, the boys' number-one supporter at Columbia, was no longer with the company. Without Greenberg championing the Jonas Brothers, the record company began losing interest in the singing siblings.

DROPPED BY THEIR LABEL

Finally, Columbia decided to drop the Jonas Brothers. The Jonas family was devastated. The record company did not think the boys had the potential to sell well. The entire Jonas family was at a loss for what to do. The boys were ready to record more songs. They already had one album out and were amassing a growing fan base throughout the country. They had learned how to perform live onstage for an audience, but without a label, it was going to be terribly difficult to make much progress. To complicate matters, the family was struggling to keep up financially. "Our savings were spent, credit cards were maxed out," explained Kevin Sr. to a reporter from People.com. "We were selling T-shirts for gasoline money at every gig."

The family was not willing to give up their dream of seeing the brothers become rock stars. It was a good thing that they stayed positive because a fantastic surprise was just around the corner. It not only changed the lives of the Jonas family, but all of their fans as well. Hollywood Records—the music division of Disney—knew about these three talented young men and was ready to offer them a contract.

CHAPTER 3

FINDING FAME

As it turned out, 2007 was a huge year for the Jonas Brothers. They had a new label, and it was one that knew exactly how to market young new musical stars. After all, Hollywood Records had succeeded in making performers like the Cheetah Girls, Miley Cyrus, and Hilary Duff household names—and big sellers. Now the company was ready to do the same for Kevin, Joe, and Nick. After their first video was aired on the Disney Channel, their fame exploded. Their fan base grew more in one month than it had in the previous two years. All of the brothers agreed that Disney was the best thing that could have possibly happened to their careers. It looked like success and popularity were straight ahead.

THE MARVELOUS PARTY

In 2007, the Jonas Brothers went on tour again. Called the Marvelous Party tour, each performance was designed to look and feel like a high school prom. Since the Jonas Brothers were homeschooled, they had missed attending their own proms, so they wanted to reenact the coming-of-age experience. Just as the tour came to an end, the Jonas Brothers' second CD was released.

This album was titled simply *Jonas Brothers*, and when Kevin Jr. was asked by Posy Edwards of Orion Books what the songs were about, he summed them up as a combination of good and bad times—plus everything in between. He added that the simple title was to let fans know the brothers were back and ready to show off what they had to offer.

The night of the album's release was a cause for celebration for the Jonas family. They had made it through the rough times and were ready to celebrate their hard-won success. Kevin Sr. rented a yacht, and the family sailed out to the Statue of Liberty in New York Harbor. It was a very special moment for the family. When *Jonas Brothers* went platinum (in other words, when it sold one million copies) in early 2008, it made all the hard work and sacrifice over the years worth it.

That year the Jonas Brothers worked extra hard to promote the album. They appeared on as many television shows as they could and played to an audience whenever possible. They performed at the

Old Disney meets New Disney as Mickey and Minnie Mouse pose for pictures with the Jonas Brothers and the Cheetah Girls at the 2008 Disney Games in Orlando, Florida.

Miss Teen USA pageant and helped hand out awards at the Teen Choice Awards. They showed up on an episode of *Hannah Montana*, performed at the American Music Awards, and had prominent spots in both the Macy's Day Thanksgiving Parade in New York City and on *Dick Clark's New Year's Rockin' Eve.* Disney executives had already decided to send Miley Cyrus out on tour—performing both her music and that of her alter ego, Hannah Montana—and now they knew who to have as her opening act: the Jonas Brothers. The three-month-long Best of Both Worlds tour began in October 2008. As soon as the Jonas Brothers returned from the tour, they released their third album, *A Little Bit Longer.* The single "Burnin' Up" hit the charts and kept climbing.

A few weeks after coming back from the Best of Both Worlds tour, the Jonas Brothers headlined their own tour called Look Me in the Eyes. The tour was named after one of their new singles. They were on the road for three months and then, after a brief summer break, they went back out on the Burnin' Up tour. On these tours their job was to pour all of their energy into their performance; since they were finally successful, they didn't need to worry about driving all night or selling merchandise to raise gas money to get to the next city. The Jonas Brothers had hit the big time. They traveled with their parents—and sometimes one of their grandmothers—as well as a full road crew.

In the "Me and Mr. Jonas and Mr. Jonas and Mr. Jonas" episode of Hannah Montana, the Jonas Brothers, Emily Osment, and Miley Cyrus rock out Disney style.

ACTING

In 2008, the Jonas Brothers' career also expanded to include act-ing in feature films. Disney wanted to make a movie showcasing

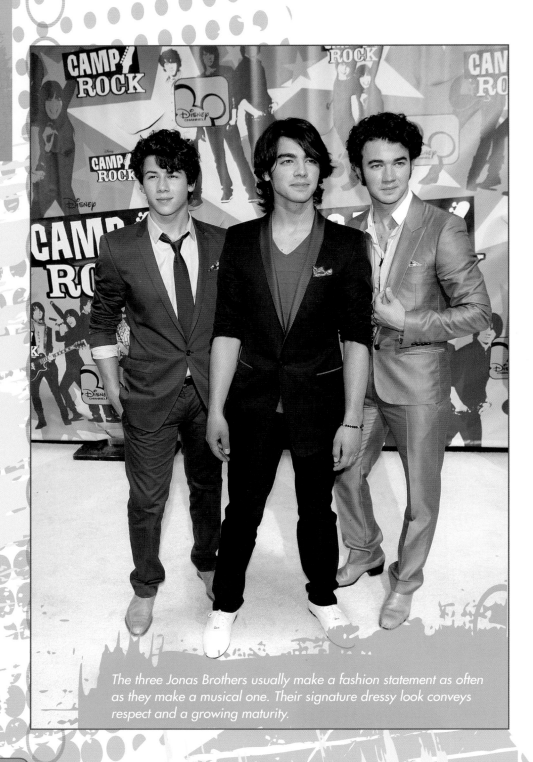

The three Jonas Brothers usually make a fashion statement as often as they make a musical one. Their signature dressy look conveys respect and a growing maturity.

some of the hottest young stars in contemporary music. The movie is called *Camp Rock*. It's a Cinderella story about a young girl whose singing talent is finally discovered.

In the film, Joe plays camp instructor Shane Gray. Kevin and Nick have roles as well. They play in the same band (called Connect Three) as Joe, but in the film they are not related. In *Jonas Brothers: Hello Beautiful*, Joe recalls the nerve-wracking experience of acting: "The biggest challenge of doing the movie was acting in general. It's so new to us. We're so used to performing onstage. I didn't know how I would do." *Camp Rock* debuted on the Disney Channel on June 12, 2008, and it proved to be extremely popular. In fact, the movie was so successful that it spawned books and other merchandise—plus a sequel.

It didn't take long for the Disney Channel to produce a documentary called *The Jonas Brothers: Living the Dream*. The film shows all of the hard work and preparation that goes on behind the scenes of a Jonas Brothers' concert. In early 2010, *Living the Dream 2* aired. This film documented the brothers as they took their music across the Atlantic and on tour throughout Europe, playing to adoring audiences all across the continent.

Next, the Disney Channel decided that the Jonas Brothers had enough fans to warrant their own television show. The executives created an idea for a series called *J.O.N.A.S.*, which stood for "Junior Operatives Networking as Spies." As originally planned, the brothers would play undercover spies who were masquerading as a rock band. The Jonas Brothers were extremely excited. "The characters are us, so they kind of have to fit our personalities," explained Nick to Scholastic Books. "We got time to meet the writers so they got to know who we were. It was cool." Kevin, Joe, and Nick were all trained in martial arts so that they could perform some of the stunts the roles called for. Their trainer, Koichi Sakmoto, was the same person who trained the actors on the television show *Power Rangers*. The Jonas Brothers were thrilled that they had the chance to work with the man who had trained the Power Rangers—they were big fans of the show.

NICK'S STORY

Nicholas was known for his boundless energy and enthusiasm. When he suddenly began acting moody, tired, and restless, his entire family knew something was wrong. Soon he started losing weight and felt irritable. In 2005, his parents took him to the doctor. After a few tests, the doctors diagnosed the problem: Nicholas had diabetes. Knowing little about the condition, his first thought was that he was going to die. His brothers were concerned, too. "On the way to the hospital, Kevin and Joe looked up diabetes online," Nicholas told Scholastic Books. "They knew more about it than I did before I got there! They're there for me all the time."

Three days in the hospital taught Nicholas everything he needed to know about handling his condition. He found out what foods to eat and not eat, as well as how to use the OmniPod, a pump that is attached to him to provide a constant source of insulin. Once Nicholas understood how to live with diabetes, he made it a priority to share that information with other kids. When the Jonas Brothers performed at the Juvenile Diabetes Research Foundation International's Carnival for a Cure, he told the world about his experience with diabetes.

But at the last minute, Disney changed its mind. The company thought that Jonas Brothers' fans would respond more favorably to a reality-based show—although the new show wasn't exactly a reality show. The television show aired as *JONAS*. It follows the story of three brothers that are struggling to balance being in a successful rock band with living their daily lives. Pursued by fans and wrestling with fame, the Jonas Brothers also take the time to be normal young people and do chores like take out the trash. Although fictional, the show is based heavily on the Jonas Brothers' experiences. It also added a new cast member: the youngest Jonas sibling, Frankie.

The show is filmed without a laugh track and using a single camera. The first episode aired May 2, 2009, and in 2010, it was picked up for a second season. Disney also announced that the title of the show would be changed to *JONAS L.A.* In its first year, it was awarded three Teen Choice Awards: Breakout Show, Breakout Star Male (Frankie), and Actor Comedy.

LINES, VINES AND TRYING TIMES

In 2009, the Jonas Brothers' fourth album, *Lines, Vines and Trying Times*, was released. It went to number 1 on the Billboard Top 200 the minute it was released. A mere ten months before, their last album also debuted at number 1. Singles like "Paranoid" and "Burnin' Up"

Earning a gold record was an important moment for the Jonas Brothers. They were thrilled when they were given one for Lines, Vines and Trying Times *in October 2009 in Panama City, Panama.*

helped catapult the album straight to the top. Weeks before the new release, the Jonas Brothers were promoting the album on Facebook and MySpace, as well as making appearances on shows such as *The Late Show with David Letterman*, *Good Morning America* in Central Park, and *The Today Show* at Rockefeller Center.

The release of *Lines, Vines and Trying Times* was followed by another world tour. Almost one million tickets were sold in the first week, and the boys played to capacity crowds in South America and Europe. The Jonas Brothers were truly on top of the world.

For those not able to attend one of their concerts, Disney released *Jonas Brothers: The 3D Concert Experience* that same year. This film captured a 2008 concert at New York City's Madison Square Garden. Moviegoers were treated to guest appearances from other musicians, including Demi Lovato and Taylor Swift. It also gave fans a chance to look at what goes on backstage and introduced them to the band's backup musicians, including guitarist John Lloyd Taylor, drummer John Cahill Lawless, keyboard player Ryan Matthew Liestman, and bassist Gregory Robert Gawbowsky. This 3-D film was the next best thing to actually seeing the Jonas Brothers live.

The film Jonas Brothers: The 3D Concert Experience was the perfect chance for fans all over the world to see the band in concert—and everything that went on behind the scenes as well.

MASSIVE POPULARITY

In just a couple of years, thanks to hard work, buckets of talent, and the right kind of company support and marketing, the Jonas Brothers went from a little-known band to one of the most popular groups in the country. They received their first Grammy nomination and won everything from an American Music Award to Teen Choice Awards. Despite the exhausting pace that they must keep up, the family continues to stay close and work as a team. Before playing a show, the three brothers get together to focus their energy. After doing their warm-ups and changing into their stage clothes, they huddle and reaffirm their love for each other and their commitment to rock. The family also takes time to pray before going onstage. Even though they are megastars, their Christian faith remains foundational to everything they do.

CHAPTER 4
GOING FORWARD AND GIVING BACK

The Jonas Brothers' religious foundation has been a part of their music from the very beginning. Although their music is not in the Christian genre, it avoids cursing and sexual references. The brothers have been part of antidrug and alcohol promotions. All three of the boys have worn purity rings, a visible statement that they will not have sexual relations with anyone until marriage. In December 2009, Kevin replaced his purity ring with a wedding ring when he married Danielle Deleasa.

As a sign of their faith and core beliefs, the Jonas Brothers all wear purity rings until the day they are replaced by wedding rings.

The group has been very vocal about the importance of their Christian faith. While it might seem strange for a rock group to also be outspoken Christians, there have been many Christian rockers. Other prominent Christian rock groups include Stryper, Creed, P.O.D., Lifehouse, and Switchfoot. Like these groups, the Jonas Brothers have struggled to balance their personal beliefs with the rock star lifestyle. It hasn't always been easy, but so far, the Jonas Brothers have been able to do it.

The history of rock music has also included a number of bands consisting of siblings. These include the Jackson 5, the Beach Boys, and the Bee Gees. Many groups also feature siblings, such as Jordan and Jonathan Knight of New Kids on the Block, Nick and Drew Lachey of 98 Degrees, Gerard and Mikey Way of My Chemical Romance, and Benji and Joel Madden of Good Charlotte. However, the Jonas Brothers have most often been compared to another homeschooled boy band—Hanson. Hailing from Oklahoma, Hanson is a trio that rose to popularity in the late 1990s with the smash hit "MMMBop." Like the Jonas Brothers, Hanson weren't just Christian rockers, they were also teen idols.

THE RISE OF CHRISTIAN ROCK

Christian rock got its start in the late 1960s and early 1970s. At this time, rock and roll was massively popular. Huge outdoor music festivals, such as the 1969 Woodstock festival in Bethel, New York, drew thousands of music fans. Christian rock was created for music fans who wanted rock and roll that emphasized wholesome values and featured lyrics in praise of God and against "sex, drugs, and rock and roll."

Around 1980, the umbrella term "contemporary Christian music" was created to encompass every style of Christian music, from pop and folk to country and gospel. Hugely popular music icons such as Johnny Cash and Bob Dylan performed religious songs at their

Even longtime hard rocker Alice Cooper has been known to perform Christian rock during his concerts. His shows sometimes include shocking things like live snakes, fake blood, and guillotines.

concerts. During the 1990s, rockers like Alice Cooper, Creed, U2, and Charlie Daniels also began performing Christian songs. Since then, the field of contemporary Christian music has continued to grow in popularity. Although the Jonas Brothers' songs do not explicitly focus on God or faith, they are definitely part of the Christian music genre.

TEEN IDOLS

With their good looks and adoring female fans, the Jonas Brothers also fall into the category of teen idol boy bands. These are groups, generally assembled by a producer, meant to appeal to a teen audience. Many boy bands don't write their own music or have much in the way of creative control over their image. Boy bands have been around, in one form or another, for decades. Groups like New Kids on the Block and 'N Sync sold millions of records and entertained millions of fans around the world, as did massive, multiplatinum groups like the Backstreet Boys and Boyz II Men. All of these groups shared a few key traits: good looks, strong harmonies, and devoted fans. The ability of the Jonas Brothers to merge Christian rock, being a boy band, and family togetherness has helped make them the powerhouse they are in the music world today. *Rolling Stone* magazine stated in a review of *A Little Bit Longer*, "The Jonas Brothers are acting their dad's age. The boys' fantastic third album is steeped in the fuzzed-up guitars, three-part harmonies and cotton-candy choruses of Big Star and Cheap Trick . . . Overall, it's a blast—as assured as any American rock album released in 2008."

CHARITY

The Jonas Brothers donate 10 percent of their earnings to a charity Nick founded in 2002. Nick was inspired to establish the program after he first saw homeless people living on the street and wanted to do something to help them. Realizing that there were many people in need of help, Nick established the Nicholas Jonas Change for the Children Foundation. Dedicated to helping children overcome adversity, the foundation is an unusual one because it encompasses five different charities. When a person donates to it, he or she can choose which one to send money to. The organization includes:

- Nothing but Nets: This program seeks to reduce malaria by providing children in Africa with mosquito netting for their beds.
- American Diabetes Association Diabetes Camp: This program pays for ten thousand children with diabetes to attend a special camp each year.
- St. Jude's Children's Research Hospital: This charity supports the work of the Diabetes Research Center.

OUT ON HIS OWN

Although he's still a full-time member of the Jonas Brothers, Nick has decided to branch out into a different music project. In February 2010, Nick released a solo album — Who I Am — with his own band, The Administration. Sometimes solo projects can disrupt the cohesion of a rock band, but not the Jonas Brothers. Nick's brothers supported the idea completely. Nick recently told Parade, "We make decisions together — even when we're doing things individually. Going into my first solo album, it's good to know that they were excited. There's been a good vibe from the get-go." According to a number of interviews with Nick, he is hoping that his solo work will go beyond earning him money and fame. This time he is looking for critical respect and perhaps, one day, a Grammy Award.

- Children's Hospital in Los Angeles: They work to earn money for the hospital's Center for Endocrinology, Diabetes, and Metabolism.
- Summer Stars Camp for the Performing Arts: This program enables teens from the ages of twelve to fifteen to pursue their dream of participating in the performing arts.

In addition to this work, the Jonas Brothers also give back to their communities in other ways. Nick has testified for diabetes research funding at the Children's Congress in Washington, D.C. Joe has run in several races to support the Special Olympics and disability rights. In addition, they have contributed to international causes, such as charities that assist in providing aid to victims of the 2010 Haiti earthquake. In April 2010, they joined TOMS Shoes for One Day Without Shoes, a program meant to raise awareness of people who live in such dire poverty that they cannot even

The entire Jonas family is dedicated to making the world a better place. They do as much as they can for a variety of charities. Here, Joe Jonas runs in a 5K race to support the Special Olympics in 2009.

afford to buy shoes. They have also been involved with the Make a Wish Foundation, which works to grant seriously ill children's wishes.

A STRONG FAMILY

More than anything else, the Jonas Brothers are about family. When they go on the road, they go together—Frankie, Denise, Kevin Sr., and the brothers' grandmother. They are definitely a tightly knit group. Their father works as their comanager. Their road manager is their uncle. Both men are pastors and commonly minister to the boys on the road.

The future is likely to hold great things for the Jonas Brothers, both as a group and as individuals. The brothers are planning concerts, appearing on television shows, landing movie roles, and putting together songs for their next album. Whatever is waiting down the road for Kevin, Joe, and Nick, it will definitely involve their close family, honor their deep faith, and be a huge success.

TIMELINE

1987	Paul Kevin Jonas is born.
1989	Joseph Adam Jonas is born.
1992	Nicholas Jerry Jonas is born.
1996	The Jonas family moves from Texas to New Jersey.
1999	Nick is cast in *A Christmas Carol* on Broadway.
2000	Frankie Nathaniel Jonas is born.
2002	Nick Jonas forms the charity Children for Change.
2005	The group goes on tour, serving as the opening act for many different performers; Nick is diagnosed with diabetes.
2006	*It's About Time* is released; the brothers go on the American Club tour.
2007	*Jonas Brothers* is released; the Jonas Brothers appear on a *Hannah Montana* episode; they embark on the Marvelous Party tour; they support Miley Cyrus on the Best of Both Worlds tour; they sign with Hollywood Records.
2008	*A Little Bit Longer* is released; the *JONAS* series airs on the Disney Channel; *Camp Rock* is released by Disney.
2009	*Lines, Vines and Trying Times* is released; Kevin Jonas gets married.
2010	Nick Jonas and the Administration release *Who I Am*.

DISCOGRAPHY

SINGLES

2002	"The Christmas Prayer"
2005	"Mandy"
2007	"Year 3000"
	"Hold On"
	"SOS"
2008	"When You Look Me in the Eyes"
	"Burnin' Up"
	"Lovebug"
2009	"Tonight"
	"Paranoid"
	"Fly With Me"

ALBUMS

2006	*It's About Time*
2007	*Jonas Brothers*
2008	*A Little Bit Longer*
2009	*Lines, Vines and Trying Times*
	Jonas Brothers: Live: Walmart Soundcheck

Kevin, Nick, and Joe Jonas released their album Lines, Vines and Trying Times in June 2009.

SOUNDTRACKS

2008	*Camp Rock*
2009	*Music From the 3D Concert Experience*
2010	*JONAS*
	Camp Rock 2: The Final Jam
	JONAS L.A.

SOLO ALBUMS

2010	Nick Jonas and the Administration: *Who I Am*

AUDITION A tryout by a singer, actor, or other performer to demonstrate his or her training or ability.

CASTING CALL A request for actors to come in and try out for a role.

CHARITY Donations of time, materials, or financial assistance to those in need.

DEMO A rough recording of a song that exists prior to its final recorded version.

DIABETES A chronic disease that impairs the body's ability to produce insulin.

DOCUMENTARY A nonfiction film about an event, issue, or individual.

GRAMMY An annual award, presented by the National Academy of Recording Arts and Sciences, Inc., to honor accomplishments in the music industry.

INSULIN A hormone produced by the pancreas that regulates the body's glucose and other nutrients.

LAUGH TRACK Recorded laughter, meant to simulate an amused audience, that is used on television comedies.

MALARIA A disease caused by mosquitoes.

MERCHANDISE Products that are sold in conjunction with a music group, such as T-shirts, books, and posters.

PLATINUM A music industry term used to describe a record that has sold one million copies.

PURITY RING A ring worn by some young Christians as an affirmation of their desire to abstain from sex until marriage.

REVIVAL A play or performance that has been brought back to the stage after a period of dormancy.

SINGLE A song that is released to gain radio airplay and promote a forthcoming album.

SOUNDSTAGE A soundproof building or room used to record music, movies, and other performances.

FOR MORE INFORMATION

American Diabetes Association
1701 N. Beauregard Street
Alexandria, VA 22311
(800) 342-2383
Web site: http://www.diabetes.org
This organization is dedicated to those living with diabetes or those
who care about them. It provides information about diabetes
research, support groups, and more.

Change for the Children Foundation
c/o The Nordinger Group
250 West 57th Street, Suite 2003
New York, NY 10107
Web site: http://www.changeforthechildren.org
Change for the Children is the charity established by the Jonas
Brothers to change children's lives for the better.

Disney Channel
3800 W. Alameda Avenue
Burbank, CA 91505
(818) 569-7500
Web site: http://www.disney.go.com/disneychannel
This television network is the home of the Jonas Brothers' popular show.

Hollywood Records
500 S. Buena Vista
Burbank, CA 91521
(818) 560-5670
Web site: http://hollywoodrecords.go.com
Hollywood Records is the Jonas Brothers' record label.

iMom.com
Family First
5211 W. Laurel Street, Suite 102
Tampa, FL 33607
(813) 222-8300
Web site: http://www.familyfirst.net
This organization is dedicated to helping mothers find inspiration,
   ideas, information, and insight. The ambassador for the group is
   Denise Jonas, the Jonas Brothers' mother.

WEB SITES

Due to the changing nature of Internet links, Rosen Publishing has developed an online list of Web sites related to the subject of this book. This site is updated regularly. Please use this link to access the list:

http://www.rosenlinks.com/mega/jona

FOR FURTHER READING

Besel, Jennifer M. *The Jonas Brothers*. Mankato, MN: Capstone Press, 2010.

DK Publishing. *JONAS Essential Guide*. New York, NY: DK Children, 2009.

Edwards, Posy. *Jonas Brothers: Hello Beautiful*. London, England: Orion Publishing, 2008.

Janic, Susan. *Jonas Brothers Forever*. Toronto, ON, Canada: ECW, 2009.

Johns, Michael-Anne. *Just Jonas!* New York, NY: Scholastic, 2008.

Jonas, Joe, Kevin Jonas, and Nick Jonas. *Burning Up: On Tour with the Jonas Brothers*. New York, NY: Hyperion Books, 2008.

Keedle, Jayne. *Jonas Brothers*. Pleasantville, NY: Gareth Stevens, 2009.

Marron, Maggie. *Jonas Brothers*. New York, NY: Franklin Watts, 2009.

Mattern, Joanne. *The Jonas Brothers*. Hockessin, DE: Mitchell Lane, 2008.

Parvis, Sarah. *The Jonas Brothers: A Biography*. Kansas City, MO: Andrew McMeel Publishing, 2009.

Ruggles, Lucy. *Camp Rock: The Junior Novel*. New York, NY: Disney Press, 2008.

Ryals, Lexi. *Jammin' with the Jonas Brothers*. New York, NY: Penguin, 2008.

Ryals, Lexi. *More Jammin' with the Jonas Brothers*. New York, NY: Penguin, 2009.

Webster, Christine. *Jonas Brothers*. New York, NY: Weigl Publishers, 2009.

BIBLIOGRAPHY

Edwards, Posy. *Jonas Brothers: Hello Beautiful*. London, England: Orion Publishing, 2008.

Harrison, Emma, and Kieran Viola. *Disney Channel Rocks!: A Companion to All Your Favorite Shows*. New York, NY: Disney Press, 2008.

Janic, Susan. *Jonas Brothers Forever*. Toronto, ON, Canada: ECW, 2009.

Johns, Michael-Anne. *Just Jonas!* New York, NY: Scholastic, 2008.

JonasBrothers.com. Various content. Retrieved April 1, 2010 (http://www.jonasbrothers.com/?content=about).

Ryals, Lexi. *Jammin' with the Jonas Brothers*. New York, NY: Penguin, 2008.

Ryals, Lexi. *More Jammin' with the Jonas Brothers*. New York, NY: Penguin, 2009.

Wolf, Jeanne. "I've Always Been Driven." *Parade*, April 18, 2010, p. 6.

INDEX

ABOUT THE AUTHOR

Tamra Orr is the author of more than 250 nonfiction books for readers of all ages. She lives in the Pacific Northwest with her four children, one husband, one cat, and one dog. She loves listening to all kinds of music and has attended numerous live concerts and stage performances over the years.

PHOTO CREDITS

Cover, pp. 1, 4 Getty Images; pp. 3 (top), 9 Jason Merritt/WireImage/ Getty Images; p. 3 (center), 14–15, 24 Scott Gries/Getty Images; pp. 3 (bottom), 12, 16 Kevin Winter/Getty Images; pp. 10–11 © Mindy Schauer/The Orange County Register/ZUMA Press; p. 18 Michael Loccisano/FilmMagic/Getty Images; p. 21 Jeff Daly/Getty Images; pp. 22–23 Joel Warren/© Disney Channel/courtesy Everett Collection; p. 27 Teresita Chavarria/LatinContent/Getty Images; pp. 28–29 Walt Disney Pictures/Zuma Press; p. 31 © The Orange County Register/ZUMA Press; p. 33 Ian Dickson/Redferns/Getty Images; pp. 36–37 Rob Hoffman/JBE/Getty Images; p. 40 Carlos Alvarez/Getty Images.

Designer: Nicole Russo; Photo Researcher: Karen Huang